I'm dedicating this book  half Graeme, he ate all months but survived.

To Tom, Molly & Emily one day you will thank me for teaching you how to perfectly "reheat" epic party food and create a show stopping family movie night.

For my Mum & Dad and their years of dedication switching off every light I left on in the house.

Contents

HELLO 4
ABOUT ME 7
SLOW COOKER RECIPES 10
   Slow Cooker Lamb Rogan Josh 12
   Slow Cooker Beef Stew 16
   Slow Cooker Meatballs 21
   Slow Cooker Beef Stroganoff 25
SOUPS 28
   Carrot & Coriander Soup 29
   Leek & Potato 32
   Tomato & Basil 35
   Winter Bean Soup 38
FAKEAWAYS 41
   Lemon Chicken 42
   Sticky Chicken 45
   Sweet & Sour Chicken 48
   Slow Cooker Doner Kebab 51
VEGETARIAN RECIPES 55
   Cheesy Taco Gnocchi Bake 56
   Sticky Hoisin Duck Stir Fry 59
   Sticky Sweet Chilli Chicken Nuggets 62
   No Cheeseburger Gnocchi 66

PUDDINGS & CAKES..69

Slow Cooker Rice Pudding 71

Waffles 74

Lemon Cake 77

Bramley Apple Baked Oats 80

Bon appetit..83

HELLO

Hello, my name is Jules and I'm the sole author of this cookbook, as you read the book you will learn more about me and my no fuss approach to cooking.

Approximately 6 years ago I had a bad fall which resulted in me damaging my spine (neck area). We all have dark times in our lives and this was mine, the pain was excruciating and my GP wasn't always very helpful.

Then came the weight gain. I gained over 3 stone in a short space of time and the impact that had on top of managing my pain was awful. I felt as though everything in my life was out of control and everything in my life was crashing down around me.

This was a really low point in my life and trying to see a way forward was near impossible.

However, we are always stronger than we realise. I went through 3 spinal operations, where I'm now left with 2 prolapsed disks, but I feel very lucky to be where I am.

During the lead up to my operation I decided I needed to change my eating habits, but the problem was I couldn't cook! We are talking about burning a pizza that just needs reheating level of cooking! I was hopeless.

Slimming World was my choice of dieting plan and I did go on to lose the 3 stone I had gained. It took time but I did it!

The learning to cook was another story. I asked my wonderful other half (I will call him this just in case he reads my book lol) Graeme, to teach me to cook. Credit to him, he has the patience of a saint, but I was still hopeless!

It became apparent very quickly that I didn't have the patience to cook and was definitely not going to be the next Nigella Lawson whom I adore.

Those long lists of ingredients filled me with terror and then the hours spent cooking the meal and watching pans boil. Nope! I had had enough! So had Graeme by this point, bless him.

Graeme is a fantastic cook no doubt about it. He loves spending time in the kitchen creating food that takes hours to prep and hours to cook. I get bored very easily and very quickly! We are two completely different cooks and that's where our cooking lessons together ended.

This is the point at which I started using my slow cooker and creating easy prep, store cupboard meals. I look at my cooking as an illusion. It may look fantastic but it's definitely a case of "smoke and mirrors".

If you look closely at my ingredients lists and style of cooking it's all tablespoons of items from jars or tins and I love it!

ABOUT ME

I'm writing this book in a style that won't suit everyone especially those who are "hot on grammar."

I want this to be written in a relaxed style and make you feel as though we're sitting at my kitchen table having a chat, as I do daily on my Facebook and Instagram accounts. I appreciate this style of writing won't suit everyone so my apologies in advance. However, I'm sure this can be overlooked with the recipes being the main focus within the book.

For me, one of the difficulties I encounter on a daily basis is getting to the end of a day and not having the energy or inclination to start cooking and I guess that's why I do most of my cooking prep first thing in the morning when my energy levels are at their highest.

The daily pain and fatigue is also another reason for using my slow cooker and as you know I will throw anything in there just to make sure there is food on the table at the end of the day.

My slow cooker has been a godsend during these years and I wouldn't be without it as I can spend 5 minutes preparing a meal, pop it in the slow cooker and walk away to get on with other jobs.

I call this my energy balancing act, I decide how much energy I have and plan my day around it. Prepping, chopping, and cooking a meal, then doing everything else that needs doing in a day can just be way too much for me, so I take shortcuts which usually means out comes the slow cooker.

My diet is based around the Slimming World plan, but I also Calorie Count at times so all recipes work within both these plans. However, this can lead to some swaps and maybe some cooking techniques that may seem a little strange at times.

These swaps and alternative cooking styles are done to reduce the "syns" (Slimming World terminology) within the recipe. When you see these swaps and techniques please do whatever you feel is best for your family or your eating plan and adjust the recipe accordingly.

An example of this would be coating chicken I miss out the flour dusting, just dip into egg, then into the crumb coating, but use whichever technique suits your cooking style best.

I have not given syn values or calories for any of the recipes within the book. The word "syn" is a protected copyright owned by Slimming World and other books written using this terminology have fallen foul of using it.

Calories can also be tricky too, if you decide to use alternative ingredients to those listed it will change the calorie value. Calories for me in any recipe are at best a guesstimate and creating a recipe within your chosen calorie counting app is always the best way to ensure the correct value.

I create what I call recipe cards, and as you move on through the book you will see that my measurements can be "a dash" "a pinch". My ingredients can be "how many you like" "use any cheese you like".

This is intentional, when I first started learning to cook if I didn't have the specific ingredients on the list it would send me into absolute panic and totally stress me out. I have learned throughout the years to just ignore most recipes and add whatever is have in my cupboards, I have also learned to adopt a very relaxed approach to cooking.

SLOW COOKER RECIPES

Me & my slow cooker go way back, and I will put my hands up in the air right now and say I will put anything in there, even mixes and sachets that are not designed to be cooked in the slow cooker, everything goes in.

I remember the look of horror on Graeme's face when I wanted my first slow cooker. He knew I didn't have a clue what I was doing, I could barely cook, never mind using a cooking gadget!

The amount of tasteless watery meals I cooked during the first 2 months were laughable. I remember reading all these fantastic recipes on Facebook and thinking how easy they sounded and went off to make them following the recipe to the letter.

Of course, they never worked because what I didn't understand was that not all slow cookers work at the same cooking temperature even if they are all set on low there is always a difference.

The size of the slow cooker can make a huge difference when following a recipe as the fuller it is the longer it takes to cook. Liquid levels in a 3.5ltr slow cooker compared to a 6ltr slow cooker are hugely different meaning the recipe may need adjusting, but of course that never even entered my head at this point.

Graeme came to the rescue, sat me down and explained the basics of using a slow cooker and how water is constantly added to the meal during the cooking process. I'm pretty sure by this time he was hoping I would just give up, because like me he was sick of eating slow cooker slop.

However, the penny dropped and here we are loving every minute of using my slow cooker and making no apologies for using it even if cooking a meal on the hob takes less time.

For me it's not about the time the slow cooker is cooking for it's the time during the day it frees up. When you are dealing with Chronic Pain daily/hourly you need to learn how and where to spend your time, and for me it's not standing cooking.

Slow Cooker Lamb Rogan Josh

This was the first slow cooker curry I learned to cook. I had wanted to cook it for months but I was so scared I would get it wrong and waste the lamb, but it turned out beautifully. Although this recipe is for Lamb Rogan Josh you can replace the lamb for chicken if you wish.

Most of the ingredients are store cupboard and I do try to keep all my recipes like this, trust me I have bought all the fancy ingredients and ended up forgetting what I bought them for and throwing them out! So, I try to keep these types of ingredients to a minimum throughout my cooking.

Heat/Spice Rating - for me this is a very mild curry but I do like spicy foods. However, it's important to understand where heat and spice in a recipe come from. Spiciness is usually from a chilli BUT people mistake heat in a recipe for spice and understanding the difference can really help when cooking a meal for your family.

Garlic - the smaller you dice or grate garlic the hotter it will become during cooking and it can really pack a punch if you add too much especially when grated. In my earlier days of cooking this was one of my worst habits and it can ruin a good meal.

Ginger - much like garlic the smaller you chop or grate it the hotter it becomes within the recipe.

My advice if you aren't keen on spicy foods is to either add smaller amounts than the recipe suggests or leave them out until the end of cooking. Once the dish is coming to the last hour of cooking, taste the sauce and decide how much garlic and ginger you want to add.

Remember any recipe is just a guide and can be adjusted to suit your family's tastes, why miss out on a great curry just for the sake of not liking garlic - simple solution leave it out.

Leaving garlic out of a curry is not traditional. However, I'm a firm believer in getting good nutritional food onto the table and to me that is more important than following a recipe to the letter.

SLOW COOKER LAMB ROGAN JOSH

INGREDIENTS SERVES 4

500g Diced Lamb OR Chicken Thighs
1 Onion
1 Tin Chopped Tomatoes
2 Garlic Cloves or 2 Teaspoons of Lazy Garlic
Half inch grated Ginger
1 Teaspoon of Ground Cumin
1 Teaspoon of Garam Masala
1 Teaspoon of Ground Coriander
1 Teaspoon of Mild Chlli
Half Teaspoon of Tumeric
Half Vegetable Stock Pot or Stock Cube
Fat Free Greek Yogurt or Natural Yogurt
 to Stir in at the end add until you get the taste you require

METHOD

Chop the onion spray a large frying pan with spray oil and soften down onions
 OPTIONAL if you don't have time then add them to the slow cooker
Finely Chop garlic if using it and grate the ginger add them to the slow cooker
Add the tomatoes
Add all spices
Add vegetable stock pot
If using lamb brown it first then add to slow cooker
Cook Lamb on low for 7 hrs if using chicken 6 hrs low
Once cooked leave to cool slightly then add yogurt

Slow Cooker Beef Stew

Beef Stew always reminds me winter is on the way and for me it's comfort food in a bowl. However, I do feel that to get a great tasting beef stew there are some pitfalls that you may want to avoid, you definitely want that warm hug in a bowl feeling from your stew.

I think beef stew is the one recipe I get asked most about and it usually goes along the lines of "it's tasteless" "it's watery" "beef is chewy". I can answer all of these with 100% confidence because I have made these mistakes when making stew in my early days. So, let me answer them for you.

It's Tasteless - this usually comes from "it's watery". The reason most stews are tasteless is because we add way too much liquid and dilute the taste of anything we put in there beyond recognition.

If you have ever watched me cook a stew, one of the first things I do is brown off the beef, now here is the rub when time is tight I don't always do this but this isn't the reason for a tasteless stew.

Browning the beef or sealing it will add flavour to the stew plus if you deglaze the pan and add those juices into the slow cooker you are really starting to build taste and flavour.

However, the biggest tip I can give to you is don't add too much liquid, a slow cooker doesn't need it.

All the vegetables you add cook down and release liquid, then there is the condensation from the lid that constantly drips liquid back into the dish you are cooking. As a rule of thumb add liquid to come approximately 5-10mm under the contents of your slow cooker.

It's Watery - just follow the rule of thumb above and don't add too much liquid.

Beef is Tough / Chewy - this is probably the easiest one to rectify all you need to do it cook it for longer.

The reason the beef is tough and chewy is it needs longer to cook, this is where I truly believe you need to "understand" your slow cooker.

I've had many slow cookers over the years and not one of them has worked and cooked in the same way. I have replaced my old Morphy Richards slow cooker with a slightly updated version of my old slow cooker and even these two don't perform at the same level.

Cooking times given for any slow cooker meal are really just a guestimate and some slow cookers will take longer and others will take a shorter amount of time, so understanding this is important.

The other factor that comes into play is the size of your slow cooker; mine is 3.5ltrs, how much liquid you fill your slow cooker with will determine the cooking time. The fuller it is the longer it will take to cook a meal.

TOP TIPS

Add lentils - if your family enjoys them, lentils are a fantastic way to help thicken up a gravy as they absorb liquid and expand during the cooking. They are also a fantastic source of protein and can really help bulk a meal out.

Add Jam - no I haven't gone crazy (just yet) sometimes when you taste a stew it can have that "metallic" taste to it or taste "too beefy" a spoonful of jam will sort that out it adds a lovely sweetness to the dish and trust me no one but you will ever know!

Cooking - wherever possible cook a stew long, slow and on low it really does result in a tastier meal.

SLOW COOKER BEEF STEW

INGREDIENTS SERVES 4

500g Diced Beef
Carrots as many as you like
1 Red Onion
1 Beef stock pot or 2 Oxo cubes
Red wine stock pot
Handful of Pearl Barley OR red split Lentils
1- 2 teaspoon of Blackcurrant or Strawberry Jam
Any vegetables you like
Water

METHOD

Chop all vegetables
In a large frying pan sprayed with oil brown the beef
BUT if you don't have time then add it to the slow cooker without browning
If you brown the beef don't forget to deglaze the pan with a drop of hot water
now add all that flavour to the slow cooker
Add onions & vegetables to slow cooker
Add Beef Stock Pot
Add Red Wine Stock Pot
Add Pearl Barley or whichever lentils you are using
Add 1 teaspoon of Jam (once meal is cooked taste gravy
 if you need more sweetness add another teaspoon)
TRUST ME THIS REALLY WORKS WELL
Add water to come just under contents by 10mm
Cook on low 7-8 hours
If you want to thicken the gravy you can add gravy granules OR take the lid off for the last hour

Slow Cooker Meatballs

If you asked me for my favourite slow cooker meal this would be right up there in my top 5. Why? Because there is just so much you can do with them, meatball subs, pasta bake, serve with spaghetti and garlic bread the list goes on.

This is a fantastic family meal, easy to make, batch cooks and freezes well. This is an all-round favourite with the kids, it ticks all the boxes.

If you have seen my most recent recipe I am using shop bought meatballs. Supermarket meatballs have come a long way since starting my blog, but if you want to make your own no problem at all.

For me, the sauce is the part of the recipe that needs to be right, not watery, tasteless or tarte.

The watery - is easy just don't add any liquid other than a tin of tomatoes or a carton of passata

The tasteless - is easy too - just follow my recipe.

The "tarte" - is the difficult one as this will depend on the tinned tomatoes you use and your taste buds.

I came across this problem when Molly was little, she hated tomatoes, but it wasn't the tomatoes she didn't like, it was the lack of sweetness. To combat this you can either add sugar, sweetener or balsamic vinegar to the sauce. Remember to always taste after cooking and adjust if needed.

Tomato based sauces and children can really be tricky and it really can just be a case of sweetening the sauce, how many bottles of tomato sauce does your child eat?? Molly loved tomato sauce but didn't like tomato based sauce meals. All it took was her dad and I to understand how much balsamic vinegar we needed to add to take the "tartness" out of the sauce.

SLOW COOKER MEATBALLS

INGREDIENTS SERVES 4

Pre Made meatballs estimate 3-4 per person depending on size OR Make your own if you like
1 Tin Chopped Tomatoes
1 Large onion
2 Teaspoon of Lazy Garlic
1 Red Wine Stock Pot
1 Oxo Cube
1 Tablespoon of Tomato Puree
1 Teaspoon of Spicentice Italian herbs
A dash of Worcestershire Sauce
A dash of Balsamic Vinegar

METHOD

Brown meatballs quickly in a red hot pan sprayed with oil this will help hold the together better in the slow cooker BUT if you don't have time skip this stage and add then without frying them off.
Add meatballs to slow cooker
Deglaze the frying pan with a splash of hot water
(Means get all the sticky bits off the frying pan)
add these juices to the slow cooker
Add tinned tomatoes to slow cooker
Chop onion & add to slow cooker
Add Red Wine Stock Pot OPTIONAL
Add oxo cube
Add garlic
Add Spicentice Italian herbs
Add a dash of Worcestershire Sauce
Add a dash of Balsamic Vinegar
Mix well
On Low 6-7 hours

Slow Cooker Beef Stroganoff

Initially I would make this on the hob, but then started to wonder would it be easier making it in the slow cooker, the answer to that is YES!

The great thing about a slow cooker, is with meals like this you can buy the cheapest cuts of beef and let the slow cooker do its thing; basically cook it for hours which tenderises the meat.

If you are using diced beef, ensure it's cooked long enough for it not to be "chewy" it needs to be melting and falling apart. I always try to cook diced beef on low for as long as possible.

Give yourself plenty of time when cooking beef, it really pays off in the taste of the finished dish.

Top tip - let the stroganoff cool slightly before adding the yogurt as you can risk curdling it especially when using a fat free yogurt.

SLOW COOKER BEEF STROGANOFF

INGREDIENTS SERVES 4

500g Diced Beef
1 Onion
1 Beef Oxo Cube
Mushrooms as many as you like
2 Tablespoons of Tomato Puree
Half Tablespoon of Thyme
2 Teaspoons Paprika
2 Teaspoons Lazy Garlic
1 Teaspoon of Wholegrain Mustard
200ml water
Fat Free Yogurt
Splash of Balsamic Vinegar
Splash of Worcestershire Sauce

METHOD

Spray pan with oil and on a high heat brown off beef
do it in batches if needed don't over crowd pan
as you will boil rather than fry
Dice Onion & Chop Mushrooms
Add beef & Mushrooms to slow cooker
Add oxo cube
Add Tomato puree
Add Thyme, Paprika, Garlic and Mustard
Add a splash of Balsamic Vinegar & Worcestershire Sauce
Add 200ml water stir well
On Low 7 - 8 hrs or until beef is cooked
Once cooked leave to cool slightly
then add yogurt stir in 1 Tablespoon and taste
 add more if needed I added 2 into mine
 but it's down to personal preference

SOUPS

I love a bowl of soup, however they aren't always the most filling of lunches mainly because you are just eating lots of blended vegetables.

As we move into the winter months, I personally need to eat more food, so if I'm having soup I either have to have a toastie on the side or add lentils to the soup. Lentils are a great source of protein and it's those proteins that will keep you fuller for longer.

Most of the soup recipes I create are either cooked in a pan on the hob or in the slow cooker, because believe it or not I don't own a soup maker!

The recipes in the book can be made using a soup maker or thrown into the slow cooker if you are busy and just want to get ahead of the day.

Carrot & Coriander Soup

Let's start off with a bit of a classic plus it is one of my favourite soups easy to make and really budget friendly.

The problem with this soup is lots of people don't like coriander so it puts them off making it.

I have chatted to many people regarding this and there really is a loathing for this fantastic herb. My response especially in this soup is have you tried reducing the amount of coriander needed and used??? Sometimes just a hint of the herb is enough to send someone over the edge but sometimes it's perfectly fine when the amount is reduced.

CARROT & CORIANDER SOUP

INGREDIENTS SERVES 4

5 - 6 Large Carrots
Half white onion
1 Large potato
1 Vegetable Stock Pot
800ml Water
Coriander as much as you like

METHOD

Chop all vegetables
In a large pan sprayed with oil soften the onion
Add carrots and potato
Add Stock Pot
Add water to come level with contents approx 800ml
Bring to boil reduce to simmer
Blend smooth
Add more water if needed
Add more coriander if needed
Season

Leek & Potato

Another classic and another firm favourite in our house but a perfect winter warmer.

In my recipe you will see I add cream cheese, usually Primula as it handles heat well, reducing the risk of it splitting, but use any cream cheese you like.

That spoonful or two of cream cheese makes all the difference to the texture and thickness of the soup, it gives luxurious thickness which feels "naughty" but in reality it is really low fat and low calories.

Leek & Potato Soup

INGREDIENTS SERVES 4

1kg of any potatoes
750g leeks
1 Vegetable Stock Pot
Approx 5-6 tablespoon of any Cream cheese I used Primula
Approx 1.2 ltrs Water
Salt & Pepper

METHOD

Chop all vegetables
Add leeks to a large pan sprayed with oil soften them down this adds flavour
Add chopped potatoes
Add Stock Pot
Add approx 1.2 ltrs of water... water needs to come approx 15mm above contents of pan
Bring to boil then reduce to a simmer
Blend smooth
Add more water if needed to get the consistency you like
Add cream cheese add as much as you like to get the taste you want
Season to taste

Tomato & Basil

I couldn't have a soup section and leave this one out as it always reminds me of the autumn months and for me always go well with a cheese toastie (but that's just me lol)

The best tomatoes for this recipe are yellow sticker ones, the squishier the better because this is when they are truly at their sweetest.

I have used vine tomatoes in this recipe which have just begun to ripen then added balsamic vinegar to sweeten the soup.

Tomatoes can always be a little "personal preference" when it comes to taste, and you may need to adjust the recipe to suit your taste especially when using tinned tomatoes.

I'm not a huge fan of over "tomatoey" tastes so I always adjust the sauce by adding either sweet or savoury ingredients which are usually balsamic vinegar (sweet) or Worcester sauce (savoury).

HOMEMADE TOMATO & BASIL SOUP

INGREDIENTS SERVES 4

4 Big fresh over ripe Tomatoes Approx 500g
1 Tin Chopped Tomatoes
1 Vegetable Stock Pot
400ml of water
A bunch of basil (add as much or as little as you like)
1 Leek
1 Tablespoon of Tomato Puree
Pinch of Mediterranean Herbs
Splash of Balsamic Vinegar

METHOD

Chop all vegetables & Basil including the stalks
In a large pan sprayed with oil soften the leek
Add fresh tomatoes and basil including the stalks to pan
Add tinned tomatoes
Add vegetable stock pot
Add a splash of Balsamic Vinegar
Add pinch of Mediterranean herbs
Add 1 Tablespoon of Tomato Puree
Add water approx 400ml but it
should cover contents by 5mm
Bring to boil then simmer until cooked
Blend smooth & taste, season with salt & pepper
NOTE If tomatoes aren't overripe the soup may not
be sweet enough add a dash more balsamic vinegar.
If you want a thinner consistency to your soup
add a little more water

Winter Bean Soup

Towards the end of 2019 I started to create a range of soup recipes called "Fuller For Longer". These soups have more power packed filling ingredients to help fill you up.

So, more proteins are added which could be in the form of beans, pulses or chicken. Then carbohydrates and vegetables to really pack in that filling power.

This soup is probably one of my favourite winter soups because again it's so easy to make and I'm pretty sure you will have most of the ingredients already in your store cupboard.

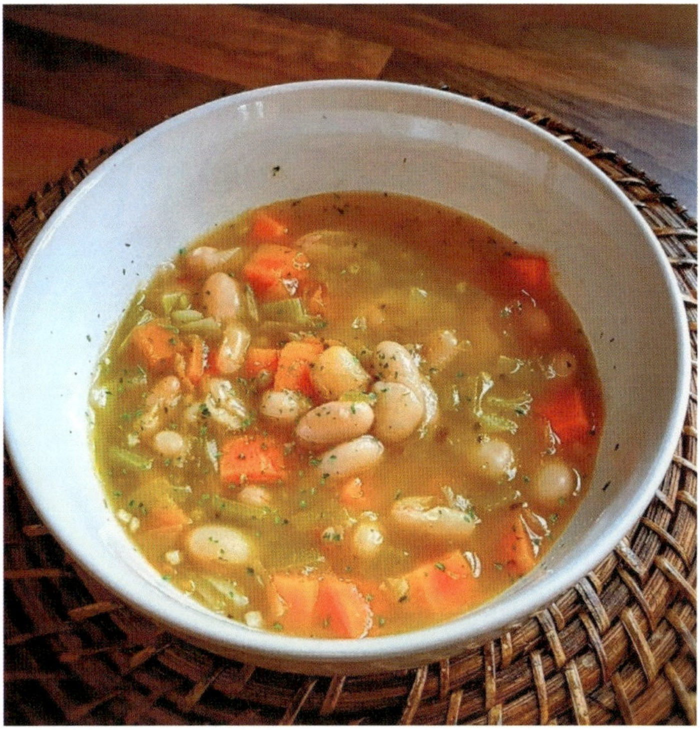

WINTER WHITE BEAN SOUP

INGREDIENTS SERVES 2

1 Can of white beans (any you like)
1 Leek or White Onion
1 Large Carrot
1 Teaspoon of Lazy Garlic
Half Teaspoon of Thyme
Half Teaspoon Oregano
1 Vegetable Stock Pot
500ml Water
Parsley to Serve

METHOD

Chop all vegetables
Spray a large pan with spray oil
Soften leek / onion
Add Garlic
Add Carrots
Add Thyme
Add Oregano
Add stock pot
Add 500ml water
Bring to boil then simmer until carrots are 90% cooked
Drain and rinse beans add them to the soup
Ensure they are heated through
Sprinkle with parsley (OPTIONAL)

FAKEAWAYS

I think this could be my favourite section within the book. I love a fakeaway and these meals really help me stick to the diet plan I follow.

Here is something I hear a lot - I have to make my family different meals because they won't eat the diet food I eat.

This can be make or break if you are trying to lose weight, cooking different meals at different times to keep everyone happy. I've tried it and failed miserably.

When I started dieting I knew I had to bring Graeme along with me and get him to "buy" into the plan I was following otherwise it just wasn't going to work. He is a real foodie and loves the variety within different cuisines.

I looked at all the food he loves and created what I call "man food" burgers, kebabs, curry, big hearty yummy tasty food, and it worked because he eats all the "diet food" cooked for him without as much as an eye twitch.

Plus, when you are craving your favourite takeaway a great homemade alternative can be a winner, not only on your pocket but your waistline too.

Lemon Chicken

Let's get the ball rolling with a firm favourite in our house such a fantastic easy family fakeaway.

The sauce for this recipe is relatively simple however it's all about patience. You need to bring the sauce together on a low heat, then turn the heat up and just take your time until it thickens.

I coated the chicken in cornflakes. Why?? It gives the best crunch ever to any coated chicken recipes but you can swap it for breadcrumbs, panko crumbs or you can leave them off altogether.

If you don't want to coat the chicken, cook the chicken in a large frying pan sprayed with oil on a low heat until it's 80% cooked through then add the sauce and follow the recipe below. A perfect way to reduce the cooking time if you are up against the clock.

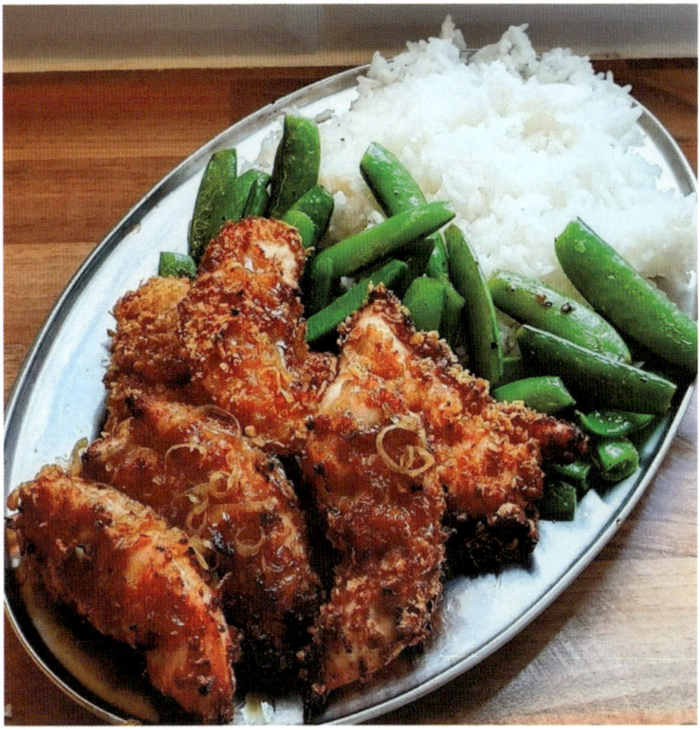

CHINESE LEMON CHICKEN

INGREDIENTS SERVES 2

2 Chicken Breasts OR chicken for 2 portions
1 Lemon
50g Cornflakes or breadcrumbs
1 Tablespoon of Soy Sauce
1 Teaspoon of Lazy Garlic
2 Teaspoon of Honey
1 Egg
1 Chicken Stock Cube
Salt & Pepper

Cut the chicken into strips or cubes place into bowl
Add 1 Tablespoon of Soy Sauce
Zest of half a lemon
1 Teaspoon of garlic mix into the chicken and leave in fridge to marinate for as long as possible
Crush the cornflakes but leave some bigger pieces don't crush them to dust
Add a sprinkle of Salt & Pepper
Dip chicken into egg then into cornflakes
Place on baking tray and spray coated chicken with oil bake in 180 degrees for approximately 35-40 mins turn over half way through
Create the lemon Sauce... make up 200ml of chicken stock
Add zest of half a lemon to stock and juice of whole lemon plus pulp of lemon, add honey mix well. Then add this to the pan
Start reducing the sauce on high heat once the sauce starts to thicken take off the heat and leave to cool slightly to let the honey set
Once reduced pour over cooked chicken

Sticky Chicken

Probably one of my favourite sauces to create as you can use it across so many different dishes. It's a great one to master as it can really help keep your weekly meal planning more interesting.

TOP TIPS - make sure the sauce is mixed properly and the honey is incorporated throughout this is really important as it will help the sauce reduce evenly.

Patience - it takes time to reduce the sauce, start on a low to medium heat bringing the sauce to a low rolling bubble. Once the sauce has started to thicken turn the heat up, the sauce should reduce quickly. Don't take your eyes off the sauce as you don't want to reduce it too far as it needs to coat the chicken.

Take the pan off the heat - every now and again to let the honey solidify, this will help you determine how much further you need to reduce the sauce by.

If the sauce needs reducing put it back on the heat and keep repeating the process until you get it to the consistency you want.

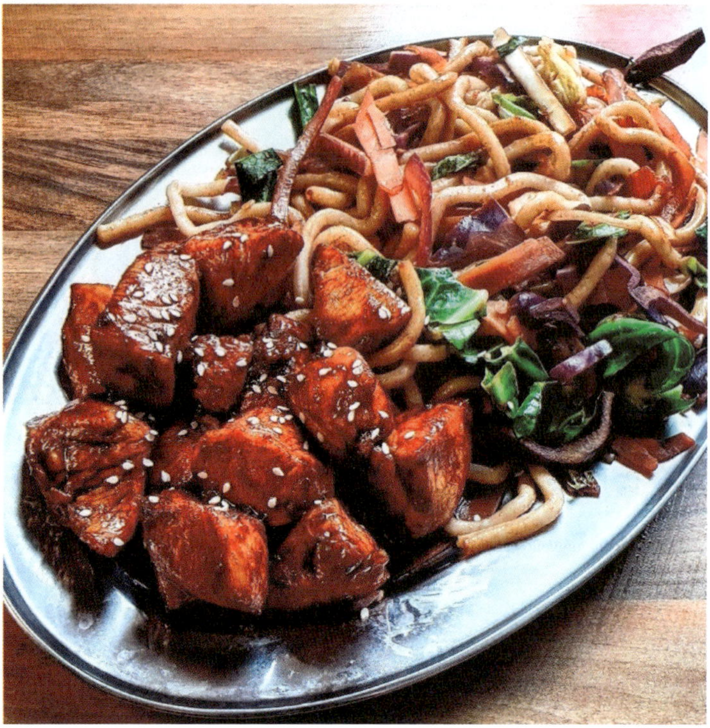

STICKY CHICKEN

INGREDIENTS SERVES 2

2 Chicken Breasts OR Diced Chicken
3 Tablespoons of Balsamic Vinegar
3 Tablespoon of Soy Sauce
3 Tablespoons of Honey
A pinch of 5 spice... OPTIONAL

If using Chicken breast dice it into cubes
Add chicken and all ingredients into a bowl mix well and leave to marinade for 30mins IF YOU DON'T HAVE TIME TO DO THIS THEN SKIP THE MARINATING STEP
In a large frying pan sprayed with oil on a low heat add the Marinated chicken
Slowly cook the chicken on a low heat
Once the chicken is cooked through by approx 80% turn the heat up to start and reduce the sauce the honey will start to create the "sticky sauce"
Reduce the sauce as much as you like but leave enough behind to coat the chicken

Sweet & Sour Chicken

I literally sweated blood and tears over this recipe to make it work for the diet plan I follow and I have to say it turned out really well and is a fantastic substitute for the real thing.

You can make this either with the breadcrumb coating or without. I have made it both ways and it's fantastic whichever method you choose.

TOP TIP - leave all the vegetables chunky, I personally feel that this helped the meal feel and taste authentic as they really do need that crunch to them.

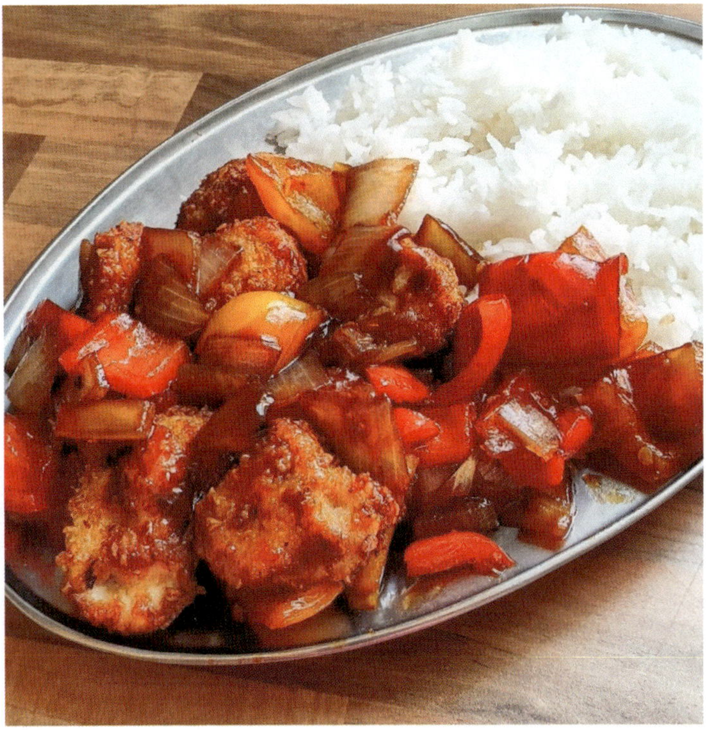

SWEET & SOUR CHICKEN

INGREDIENTS SERVES 2

2 Chicken Breasts OR equivalent
3 Tablespoons of Soy Sauce
4 Tablespoons of White Wine Vinegar
4 Tablespoons of Sugar / Sweetener
5 Tablespoons of Tomato Ketchup
50g of Cornflakes or Breadcrumbs
1 egg
1 white onion
2 peppers any colour you like
Salt and pepper

Dice chicken into cubes & Chop all vegetables but keep them chunky
Crush the cornflakes add a sprinkle of Salt and pepper
Dip chicken into egg then into cornflakes you are only looking for a light coating
Into oven 180 degrees for 15-20 mins turning halfway
In a large frying pan sprayed with oil soften the onion for 10mins then add the peppers cook for another 5 mins all vegetables need to still have a crunch to them.
Make the sauce using soy, vinegar, ketchup and sugar mix it well and taste it if happy add it to the vegetables if not adjust to suit your taste usually this means, add more ketchup and vinegar, on a medium heat keep stirring the sauce will start to thicken.
NOTE don't reduce the sauce too far down as you need it to coat the chicken
Add baked chicken to frying pan and coat with sauce

Slow Cooker Doner Kebab

I had to sneak this one into my top favourites fakeaway recipes, it's such a family favourite BUT also super easy to make.

If you have not tried cooking a kebab in the slow cooker give it a try, it works well and it frees up your time to get on with other things whilst it's cooking.

TOP TIP - understand how hot your slow cooker works, this is something I try to instil on everyone who owns a slow cooker it will really help with cooking times.

Understanding your slow cooker - the only way to do this is cook meals and keep a log of how long a recipe takes to cook, for example meatballs - in my slow cooker 3.5 ltrs on low this will be cooked in 6 hours.

My slow cooker works slightly on the hotter side even when on low. If your slow cooker cooks this recipe in 4-5 hours on low you will need to adjust the recipe, if your slow cooker takes 7 or 8 hours to cook the recipe again adjust accordingly.

All slow cookers don't heat at the same rate so giving out cooking times can be really hit and miss, understanding how yours works and how quickly it cooks on a low setting can be a huge advantage.

If you overcook the meat it will become dry and crumble, use a digital meat thermometer to check the internal cooked temperature once it's reached the kebab is cooked.

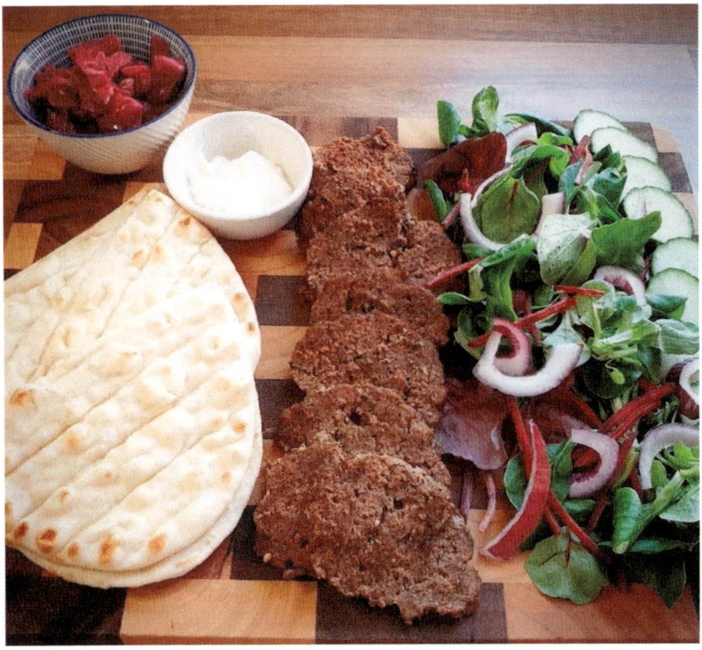

SLOW COOKER DONER KEBAB

INGREDIENTS SERVES 4

500g 5% Fat Free Minced Beef
1 Teaspoon of Paprika
1 Teaspoon of Cumin
1 Teaspoon of Dried Mint
2 Tablespoons of Garlic
1 Beef Oxo Cube
Half a teaspoon of Onion Powder
A pinch of Salt & Pepper
Tin Foil

Add mince to mixing bowl
Add all spices
Crumble in oxo cube
Add a pinch of Salt & Pepper
Mix well by hand ensure the spices are distributed evenly as possible
Place the mince onto tin foil and form a Kebab shape wrap the foil around the Kebab
Add approx 10mm water to slow cooker
Scrunch up foil to form 2 foil balls
Add the foil balls to the slow cooker, sit the Kebab on top of them
Cook on high 4 hrs

VEGETARIAN RECIPES

I really got hooked on "Meat Free Monday" and have loved all the recipes I have created.

Creating new vegetarian recipes is still something I want to keep doing and will keep doing, as you can imagine it's a juggling act with time at the moment.

As with any recipe you can adapt it to include meat or exclude meat, so if like me you are a meat eater don't let this section put you off just swap out the vegetarian option to your preferred meat.

There are so many fantastic meat free alternatives in the supermarkets and the ranges just seem to be going from strength to strength.

If you haven't tried dedicating one day a week to a vegetarian meal, then maybe try it. I can promise you won't be disappointed.

Cheesy Taco Gnocchi Bake

When I first floated this recipe idea past Graeme he really did look at me as if I was mad and I can't say he was 100% sold on the idea either.

Oooh how wrong he was! This recipe does sound crazy but it works so well.

I've had so much positive feedback regarding it, even from little fussy eaters, which is always great to hear. I know how testing children can be with eating and trying different foods.

If you aren't sure about using gnocchi, swap it for pasta, gnocchi is potato dumplings and can be found in the chilled isle fresh, or near the pasta, cooked.

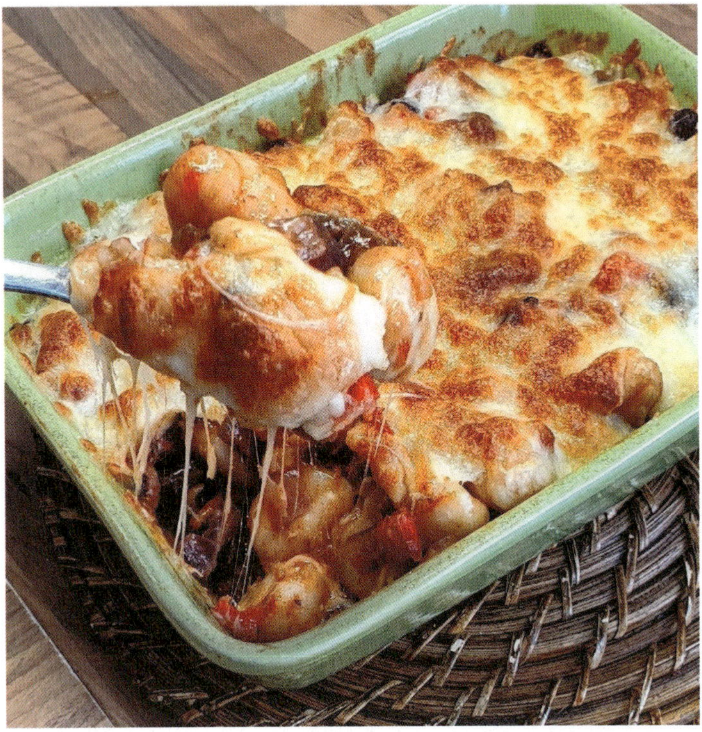

CHEESY TACO GNOCCHI BAKE

INGREDIENTS SERVES 3-4

500g Gnocchi Fresh or Cooked
1 Tin Taco Beans in Tomato Sauce
Any Vegetables you like i used mushrooms, peppers and a red onion
Any Cheese you like
Any spices you like i added 1 teaspoon of Paprika BUT Smoked Paprika would also work well in this recipe. THIS IS OPTIONAL YOU DON'T NEED TO ADD

Chop all vegetables
In a large frying pan sprayed with oil soften the onion
After 15 mins add the peppers and mushrooms or whatever vegetables you are using
Add the Taco beans
In a large pan of boiling water add the gnocchi it takes minutes to cook. It's cooked when it floats to the top REMOVE it and drain immediately and don't over cook it.
Add gnocchi to frying pan with vegetables and beans mix well
Add cheese to top and pop under a grill. until. cheese is melted

Sticky Hoisin Duck Stir Fry

This was AMAZING such a fantastic easy recipe, I used Linda McCarteny frozen duck, I've never used it before but we loved it. The texture was brilliant and it cooked well with bags of flavour.

You can use duck breast or leg in this recipe if you wish for all the non vegetarians, but I would highly recommend you try this vegetarian option.

The duck I used cooks from frozen making it a perfect quick meal. It literally cooks in 5 minutes.

I served mine with a stir fry and it worked beautifully, but you could use this duck as part of a bigger fakeaway meal and make duck wraps.

TOP TIP - Don't let the duck cook for too long as the edges start to go crispy and once they get to this stage they can be really tough to eat.

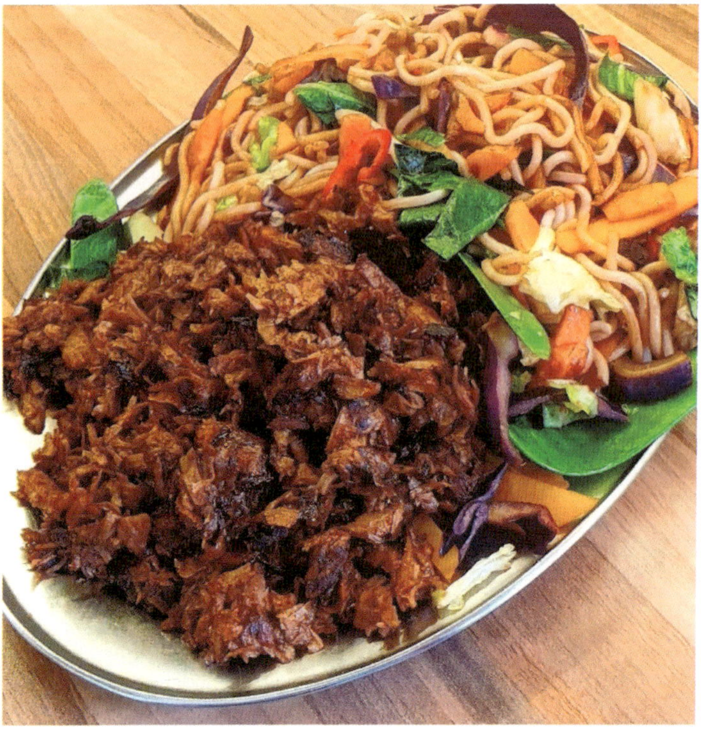

STICKY HOISIN DUCK STIR FRY

INGREDIENTS SERVES 2

300g Vegetarian Shredded duck OR 2 duck breast / legs
1.5-2 Tablespoons of Hoisin Sauce
1-2 Tablespoons of Soy Sauce
Any stir fry vegetables you like
Any Noodles you like

In a large frying pan sprayed with oil add the vegetarian duck this is cooked from frozen on a medium heat for 6-7 mins try not to let the duck get "too crispy"
If using Duck breast / Leg cook in pan or in Grill / Grill pan or oven. Once cooked shred with 2 forks.
Add 1.5 Tablespoons of Hoisin Sauce to the duck mix well
Add 1 Tablespoon of Soy Sauce to the duck mix well
Now taste you may want to add a little more Hoisin or soy sauce but adjust to your taste
In a 2nd pan sprayed with oil add the stir fry vegetables cook until slightly soft add a dash of Soy sauce
Cook your noodles as per packet instructions then add to the stir fry vegetables add another dash of Soy sauce

Sticky Sweet Chilli Chicken Nuggets

A recipe born out of pure laziness and I'm making no apology for telling you that.

Sometimes I think we over complicate cooking and it's usually the simplest easiest meals that are the best ones. So here is mine so simple I should be ashamed to put it in here, but so brilliant it deserves a spot.

Use any chicken nuggets you like either vegetarian or not but definitely give this one a try.

TOP TIP - The sauce needs to reduce to ensure it has a sticky texture so start on a low heat and make sure all ingredients are combined.

Bring the sauce to a low rolling bubble then after a couple of minutes turn the heat up the sugars in the chilli will start to caramelise and the sauce will reduce quickly at this point.

Take the pan off the heat and let the sauce solidify, this helps you determine how thick the sauce is and how much further it needs reducing.

Taste - I cannot emphasise this enough when following a recipe as our taste buds are all different, some people are more receptive to sweet tastes and some to savoury.

Taste the sauce and ensure it's to your liking, you may want to add more sweet chilli or more soy, this is the sweet and savoury within this recipe.

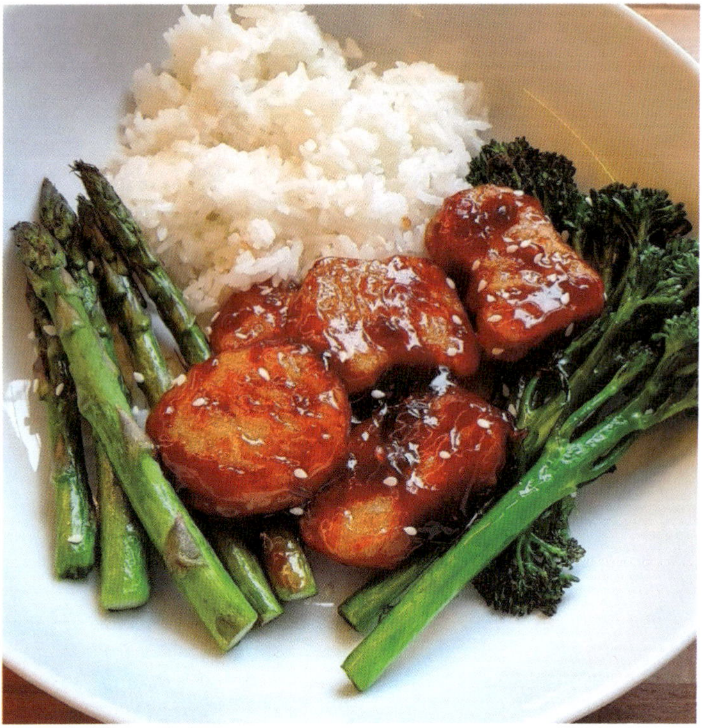

STICKY SWEET CHILLI CHICKEN NUGGETS

INGREDIENTS SERVES 2

6-8 Quorn Chicken Nuggets OR Any Chicken Nuggets you like
Half OR 1 Tablespoon of Soy Sauce
2 Tablespoons of Sweet Chilli Sauce

Cook the chicken nuggets according to the manufacturer instructions
In a large frying pan add half a tablespoon of Soy and 2 Tablespoons of Sweet Chilli bring to a low simmer
Reduce the sauce until it becomes thick and sticky this doesn't take long so don't take your eye off the pan
TASTE the sauce adjust to your taste add more soy or more sweet chilli
Add the cooked chicken nuggets to the pan and coat with them with the sauce

No Cheeseburger Gnocchi

I must admit this one sounds ridiculous even to me, but on social media there are so many Cheeseburger Pasta recipes I thought I would adapt one and make it vegetarian.

I used plant based sausages from our local supermarket but you can use any sausages you like or any vegetarian mince you like.

Again, if you are unsure of using gnocchi then swap it for pasta or rice both would work equally well.

In the ingredients list for this recipe I have used Spicentice Gourmet Burger Blend, I make no apology for loving Spicentice products they are so easy to use and packed full of flavour.

Obviously not everyone will have this spice so you can substitute it for a supermarket burger blend. I find the difference between the spices I use and the supermarket spices is the potency of the blend. Sometimes the ones from the supermarket can lack something.

However, as I always say in my live cooking sessions, use whatever you have and if you would like to try Spicentice I'm pretty sure you will love them as much as I do.

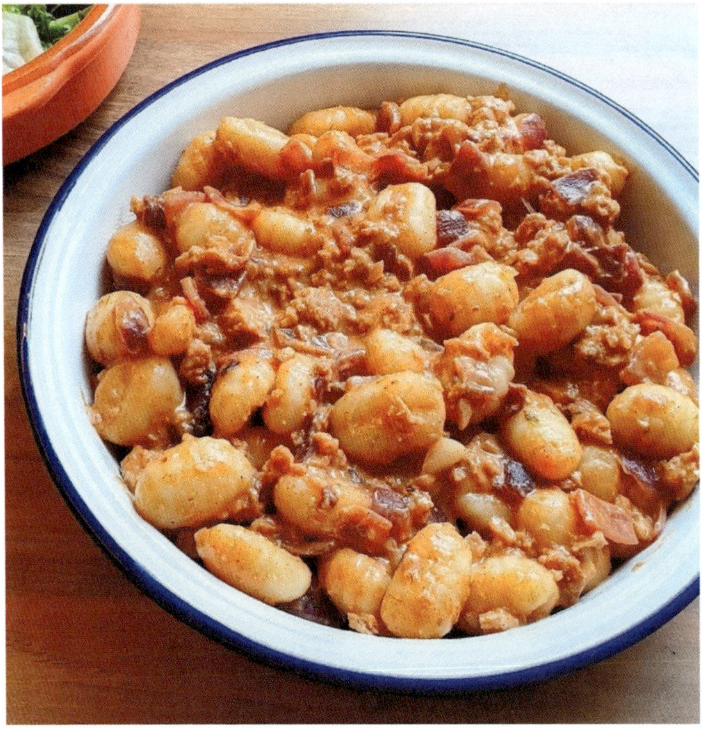

NO CHEESEBURGER GNOCCHI

INGREDIENTS SERVES 3

500g of Gnocchi
3 Meat Free Sausages OR Quorn mince
1 onion
1.5 Tablespoons of Passata
1.5 Teaspoons of Spicentice Gourmet Burger Rub from www.spicentice.com use discount code JULES20 for 20% off any order AFFILIATE
3-4 Tablespoons of any Cream Cheese you like
Hendersons Relish
Half Vegetable Stock Pot
NOTE YOU CAN USE MEAT VERSIONS OF THE ABOVE IF YOU WISH

Dice onion Spray a pan with oil and soften onion
Add sausages or Quorn to pan cook for a couple of minutes if using sausages break them up to resemble a mince texture
Add half a vegetable stock pot
Add 1.5 Teaspoons of burger seasoning
Add 1.5 Tablespoons of Passata
Add 3-4 Tablespoons of Cream Cheese
Add a splash of Hendersons relish
Add a splash of water to the mix to create the creamy sauce
Cook Gnocchi in a large pan of boiling water when it floats to the top its cooked drain immediately add it to the creamy burger mix
Ensure the gnocchi is coated in the creamy mixture if the mixture is too dry add a splash of water

PUDDINGS & CAKES

This is probably going to be the section that will cause the most controversy.

The cakes and puddings in this section fit with the diet plan I follow, therefore they are low in fats and sugars, so this can make the texture slightly different to what you are used to.

I have made all these cakes and pudding many times and although not traditional, are still really tasty and definitely worth trying especially if you are trying to lose weight.

Let's talk about the "sweet tooth". I don't particularly have one, don't get me wrong every now and again I love a slice of cake but not everyday or even every week.

Graeme is the one that has the sweet tooth which I found challenging when we were both at the beginning of our diet journey.

These recipes did help combat the need for something sweet, but remember everyone's taste buds are different and I would suggest you taste the mixture of each recipe and if needed add more sweetener or sugar.

I don't use sugar or sweetener in my tea or coffee and try not to use it in any of my baking, I don't even use it on cereal.

A great alternative is zero sugar coffee syrups, these work well when trying to substitute sweetener or sugar.

You can find them in many online stores and they come in every flavour imaginable.

Slow Cooker Rice Pudding

Probably my favourite recipe ever to make as it is all thrown into the slow cooker and when it's cooked it has a lovely creamy texture.

You can use any milk you like and if you wish, you can add sweetener or sugar to the rice pudding, as you will see the recipe doesn't list sweetener in the ingredients. I find the sweetness level right for me, this recipe is a perfect example of tasting and adjusting to suit your taste.

TOP TIP - Once the rice pudding is cooked remove it immediately from the pot as the residual heat will keep cooking the rice and the rice will keep absorbing the milk.

If the pudding becomes a little too thick just add more milk. You can batch cook this recipe and freeze it too.

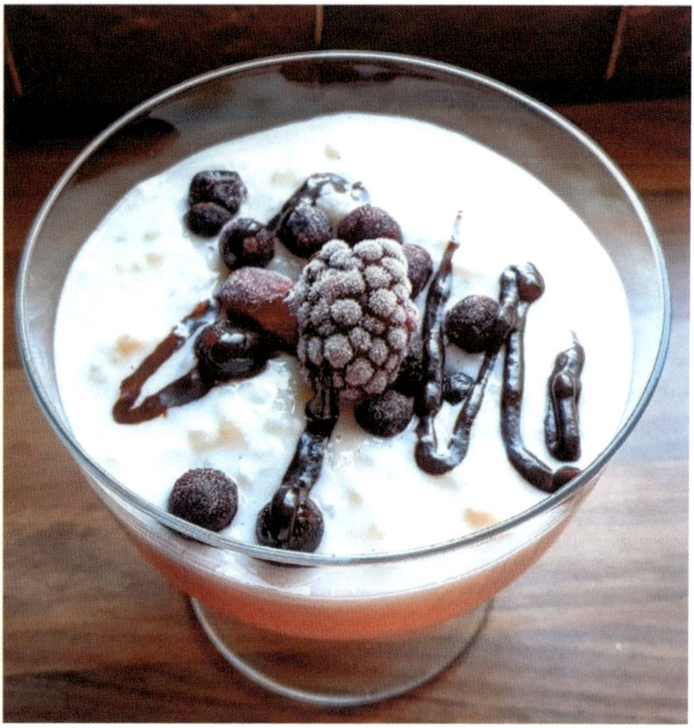

SLOW COOKER RICE PUDDING

INGREDIENTS SERVES 4

150g Pudding Rice
1 ltr of milk any milk you like
Use sweetener or sugar if you like, I used a sugar free flavoured coffee syrup to sweeten & flavour mine
Any flavourings you like

Add Rice & Milk into Slow cooker
Cook on high 3- 4 hour ish OR on low 5-6 hrs
Once cooked add your flavourings
Remove from slow cooker immediately as the residual heat will keep cooking the rice and it will keep absorbing the milk.
If you overcook the rice and it becomes too thick add more milk
You can portion this and freeze if you are batch cooking it.

Waffles

Who doesn't love waffles? These are usually my "go to" breakfast as they are super filling.

This it's not a traditional waffle recipe as this fits in with the diet plan I follow but don't let that put you off, they are really tasty and definitely worth trying.

I don't blend the oats but if you want a smooth texture in your waffles then blend to a powder like consistency.

Electric waffle machines are fantastic as you don't need to wait for the oven to heat to temperature, however I have used silicone waffle moulds which work equally as well.

Batch cooking is key here and I usually make a huge batch then freeze them to reheat pop in a toaster or under a grill.

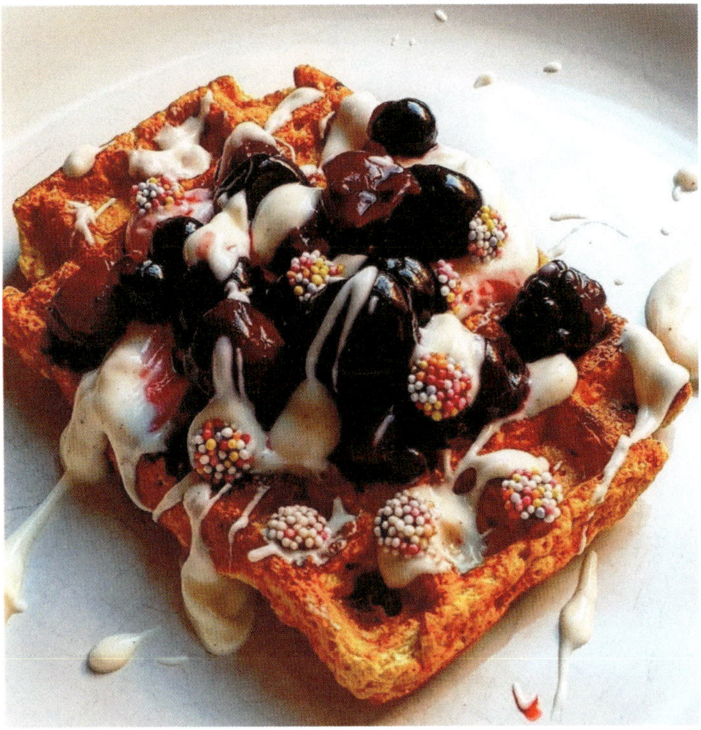

Sweet Waffles

INGREDIENTS SERVES 1

40g Porridge Oats
1 egg
2 Tablespoons of Fat Free Yogurt
Any flavourings you like
Any sweetener you like

Enter your Add all ingredients into a mixing bowl
Make sure everything is combined
Add waffle mixture to an electric
Waffle maker or into a silicone waffle mould and cook until firm to the touch
You can batch cook these and freeze
To reheat pop in a toaster or under the grill

Lemon Cake

When reading this recipe you will probably wonder where all the flour and butter is, but this is another example of moulding a recipe to suit a diet plan.

I have made this cake many times and it is beautiful and light, it's not a traditional cake texture but nonetheless it will really help when you need something sweet to eat.

TOP TIPS - When mixing the egg white mixture into the flour and eggs take your time and add only 1/3rd of the egg whites to begin with. This really helps the two mixtures bind together but also makes it easier to incorporate the egg whites.

Try not to mix too hard when adding the remaining egg whites as you don't want to "knock" the air out of the flour and egg mixture. It's this airy mixture that helps the cake rise.

If you can see egg white trails through the mixture it's not combined enough and you will have an "eggy taste" to your cake, have patience at this stage it will pay off in the tasting.

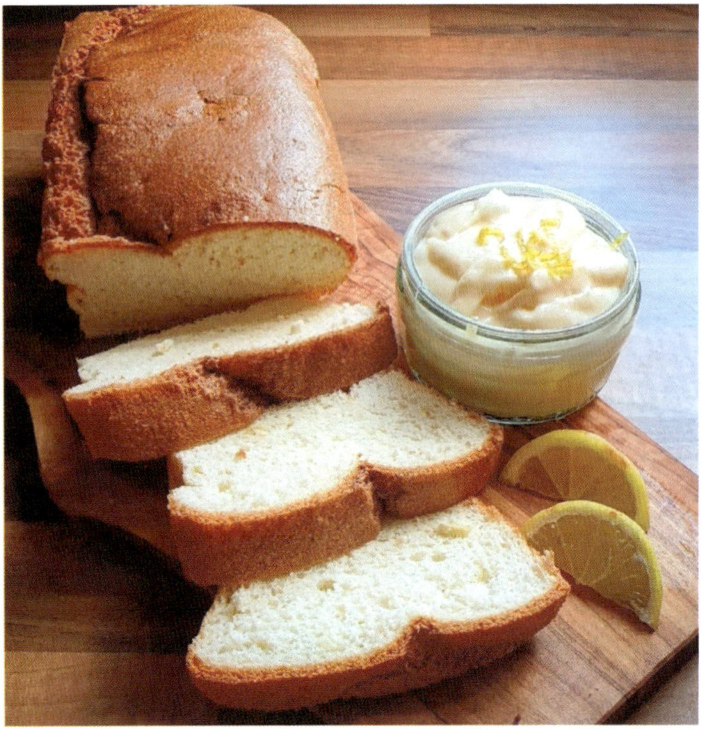

LEMON CAKE

INGREDIENTS

50g Self Raising Flour
5 Eggs
15g of sweetener
2 Lemons

Sieve flour into bowl
Separate eggs add yolks into flour
Add whites into a separate bowl
Add sweetener to flour & yolks
Add Zest of 2 Lemons into flour mixture
Add juice of 1 lemon into flour mixture
Mix well ensure everything is incorporated TASTE add more lemon if needed Add more sweetener if needed.
Whisk the egg whites into stiff peaks
Add 1/3rd of the egg whites to the cake mix and incorporate it slowly try not to "knock the air" out of the egg whites. Now add the rest of the mix and again slowly mix it through
NOTE MAKE SURE THERE IS NO EGG WHITE MIXTURE SHOWING HAVE PATIENCE AND ENSURE ITS ALL MIXED THROUGH PROPERLY
Place mixture into oven proof dish and bake on 180 degrees for approx 20-30 mins depending on your oven
Ensure cake is cooked through use a cocktail stick or similar to test

Bramley Apple Baked Oats

A filling breakfast which can be made using any combination of flavours, bramley apple is my favourite.

You can blend the oats if you like to achieve fine texture in your baked oats.

When I first started my diet journey I wasn't overly keen on baked oats, it was the texture I didn't like. I will call it "squidgy" and that type of centre really isn't my cup of tea.

However, I found if I baked them for slightly longer the middle was a little firmer and I actually did enjoy them.

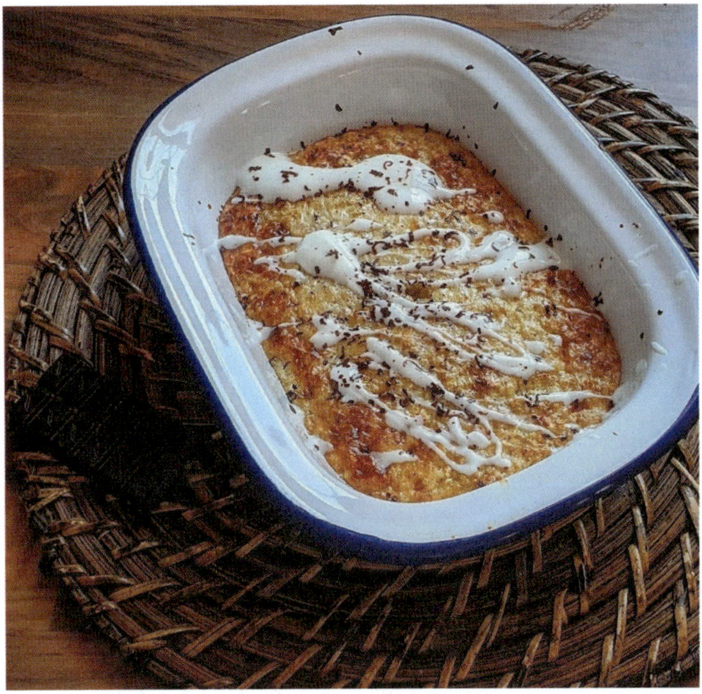

BRAMLEY APPLE BAKED OATS

INGREDIENTS SERVES 1

40g Porridge Oats
1 Egg
1 Tablespoon of Apple Sauce
2 Tablespoons of Fat Free Yogurt
Pinch of baking powder (optional)

Add all ingredients into a bowl and mix well
I haven't added any sweetener as the apple sauce is sweet enough
Taste the mixture and add sweetener if you like
Fill ovenproof moulds with half the mixture
Add half a tablespoon of apple sauce into each mould
Fill mould with the mix you have left
Bake on 180 for 15-20mins
NOTE I LIKE MY OATS BAKED FIRM AS I DON'T LIKE MINE TO HAVE A SQUIDGY TEXTURE IN THE MIDDLE IF YOU ARE LIKE ME BAKE THEM FOR APPROX 25-30 MINS

Bon appetit…………………..

And there we have it, my first ever cookbook. This is only a small selection of the recipes from my website, I have so many more I would love to share with you.

This process has been terrifying and exciting all at the same time, but I really hope in some way these recipes help and inspire you to try some of them out.

Until the next time, Love Jules xx

@julesthelazycook_sw

Jules The Lazy Cook

www.julesthelazycook.co.uk

I decided to add more into the paperback version, mainly because the way Amazon print the book.

There are some transformation pictures of me which I hope will help you see you can lose weight no matter what you encounter.

Plus, different serving suggestions for the meals within the book

Picture on the left was before my first spine operation, although I'm smiling, I felt like crying when I saw this picture.

Picture of the left was the one that started my journey, when I'm having a "diet wobble" I take a look and it and remind myself how far I've come

The man behind the scenes and my biggest inspiration and my number 1 supporter.

Sweet & Sour Chicken, in this version I haven't coated the chicken in breadcrumbs. As you can see it still works perfectly well.

Gnocchi Taco Bake – I had lots of carrots that needed using so added them into the recipe.

As you know I hate wasting food therefore I will add anything that needs using up.

My obsession with anything cheese! Soup and a toastie is always a winner.

This is how I ensure I'm full when eating a bowl of soup, I always add something on the side.

Sticky Gammon – In my Sticky Chicken recipe, I talk about how this sauce can keep meal planning interesting and help to vary your weekly meals.

This is a great example, same sauce but I swapped chicken for gammon (ham). You can used leftover cooked gammon (ham) in this recipe just add everything into the pan at the same time.

Sticky Sweet Chilli Nuggets – Quickest meal ever to make, in this suggestion I have used microwave pouch rice which cuts down the cooking time.

Never be afraid of using microwave rice if you are short on time, no one will every know.

Slow Cooker Meatballs – when trying to lose weight adding as many vegetables as possible is important.

They are a great source of fibre and have real filling power.

When I make spaghetti and meatballs, I use courgette spiralized to reduce the amount of spaghetti I'm eating.

Its also a fantastic way of increasing your vegetable intake.

Sticky Chicken – served with microwave rice and potato wedges and a side of crunchy vegetable.

Creating that "half chips half rice" fakeaway.

Slow Cooker Beef Stew – sneaking in those vegetable this time within the potato. Leek and potato mash a real favourite of mine.

Slow Cooker Beef Stew – again adding more vegetables by serving with carrot & turnip (swede) mash instead of potatoes

Slow Cooker Beef Stew - with pie lid, you can still eat what you love when dieting just maybe less of it.

Pasty is notoriously high in calories, but I love it so rather than not have it I just reduce the amount I use.

Sticky Prawns – again using the sticky chicken sauce recipe but swapping chicken for prawns.

Waffles – I have an electric waffle machine, but I have used silicone waffle moulds that you use in the oven.

This is how they look after they are baked.

And that really is it from me this time, I hope you have enjoyed the extra pages added.

Printed in Great Britain
by Amazon